Fish Head & Grits

Valerie Seymoure

Fish Head & Grits

INTRODUCTION

I remember growing up in a three-family house and I had two sisters and three brothers. I was the baby for a long time. Every summer, my dad would take us to Valley Fair to buy us tables and chairs for the backyard. We would have so much fun. We used to get into our pool and sip on Kool-Aid. We had games like old maid. Our dad used to always cheat by putting the old maid higher so I would be the one who picked her.

Mom used to always buy us clothes from the thrift store. I remember I had an old fuzzy hat that I wore to school. The kids teased me all the time about it. I didn't want to wear the hat anymore. I remember my mom used to walk us to school in the morning and I couldn't wait for school to be over because she would be there waiting for me afterward. My mom did not work. She was a stay-at-home wife.

My dad wore plenty of hats. He was a fire fighter, a police officer, and the paramedic. I remember he always kept his firefighter boots on the back porch. They were taller than me. I remember being the youngest at the time. I used to sleep with my parents. We used to ask daddy for money when he came home. He would say, "Go get my pants off the dresser." He always wore polyester pants with a belt that was heavier than me. I remember we'd get so much candy for a nickel. Nowadays, you pay a quarter for one fish.

Valerie Seymoure

One night as I snuggled up with my mom with my thumb in my mouth, I felt something touching me that was extremely uncomfortable. It was my dad at the foot of the bed touching me inappropriately. My little feet were kicking as hard as they could. The next morning when I woke up, I told mommy what daddy did. Thinking that she would come to my rescue, I quickly found out this was not the case.

Mommy treated me like I was the girlfriend. All the walks from school were no more. She stopped giving me the attention that a six-year-old needed. Everyone in the house knew what daddy did, and they teased me about it. That is where the seed of low self-esteem came from. I was seven years old. My mom had another baby. She was so beautiful. All the attention I needed? I would never get at this point.

I remember the house being so cold because we had no heat, there was this one radiator with an old raggedy couch that everyone stood in front of. Every time you were managing to get to the radiator, the spring of the couch would scratch you. One day, dad didn't come home at night. In the morning, we heard a knock on the door. Mom and I ran down the stairs. Mom had fire in her eyes because she knew it was dad.

I stood at the bottom of the stairs. When Mom opened the door, she said Butch, where have you been? As she opened the door, he came in. He saw a wooden chair with metal legs on it and picked it up and slammed it right over her face. That just brought tears to my eyes.

Fish Head & Grits

I didn't know what to say or do. As I write this book, I am healing. I used to always go to the store and the laundromat to wash the rugs. I noticed that made my mother happy. She liked seeing the house clean. Come to think of it, I never saw mommy smile. Wow! My mother's self-esteem was so low because my father would call her all kinds of filthy names like buzzard. This was domestic violence at its worst. She took care of six kids without a job. There were times where we did not have hot water. But there were days when we did have water, we had to boil it and put it in the tub.

We did the same for the dishes. When I was eight years old, I went to the store to buy some milk. I cross the street and got the milk, but as I was coming back, I was struck by a car. All I remember is the smelling salt waking me up on the ground. They rushed me to Beth Israel Hospital. My right leg was sprained, and I was in severe pain. After being treated at the hospital, my dad made me limp all the way home with my injuries. From the hospital, we walked from one street to another. How horrible!

I remember daddy came home from work one night and he was losing his mind. He told us that when they responded to a call, they had to do CPR on whoever. This case that he had to do CPR on was a dead infant. It triggered something in him. The family and house really went down from this experience. I used to always find my mom looking out the window singing, "I found love on a two-way street." She used to cook well, but somehow always manages to burn everything.

Valerie Seymoure

We went from going food shopping to getting scrap from wherever. I remember we would go to the fish store to get mommy's porgies, but things were tough. My dad and I went to the fish market for fish. I would be amazed to see lobsters in the tank swimming. This day, we walked pass the porgies that was lying on the ice. We walked past the whiting fish, which I loved. We passed the shrimp and then the crabs that were still moving in the crates. Dad met Charlie. He was the butcher. Charlie used to clean and gut the fish. I notice we didn't buy any fish that day. We were standing where the process of getting the fish ends. Dad said thanks to Charlie and took a big garbage bag full of scrapings that Charlie threw away.

It was dinner time, but I ran upstairs to sit down to eat something on my plate that was looking back at me. It smelled good, but it looked scary. It even had a tail at the end. In the middle you can still see the plate because the fish had no meat on it. It was all bones, and on the side were hot grits. This became normal in our household. I remember my dad used to bring this little baby to the house, and she was dirty and smelled terribly, but my mom would change her and do her hair.

That said a lot about her. Come to find out years later, she was our sister. I also had another sister whose name was Angie. It seems as if the black mother would get pregnant every year. I remember mommy went into labor and we were all excited to meet our little sister. A week later, mommy came home, and we wondered… where was the baby? There was no baby. Mom explained that she went into labor and the doctors said that the baby's shoulders was too big, and the doctor broke the babies' neck.

All she could remember is the baby's head was dangling between her legs. The hospital kept the baby for weeks to do an autopsy. Mom was so distraught. My parents decided to have the funeral for the baby. They took me and my sister to the graveyard. I didn't know what to expect as I walked on the dry dead grass in the cemetery. As I approached this little propped up white box, it contained my little sister. She was dressed in all white with the most beautiful outfit on. Back then, bonnets were in. As I looked at the beautiful face and her fat cheeks, I noticed something orange that was smeared on her dress. It was her skin. They kept her body too long, until it started to decay. Why did they allow me to see that?

When I was ten years old, we got a new tenant on the third floor – a lady with two children. The young lady was probably in her 40's. Her sons were 17 and 16 years old. At my home, no one really watched me because they never had time due to other things that were going on in their lives. I remember the 17-year-old would tell me to meet him on the back porch. He had something for me. As a child, you don't really understand what's going on. He had lots of candy and gum for me, but all I had to do was stroke him up and down and hold it for a few seconds with my hands full of white stuff.

I didn't understand what was going on, but I knew I couldn't wait to get that candy. At around the age of ten, I had a friend, and her birthday was August 9th. I used to go to her house because I knew they would celebrate by saying happy birthday and just to see her gifts and beautiful birthday cake. Mommy told me my birthday was the same day as Lucille's birthday. That's why I was so excited for her birthday. I noticed that everyone had a birthday party except me. Every year we would clear out the backyard for everyone's birthday, except mine.

As I got older, I realized on my birth certificate, I saw I was born on August 27th. So, all the years that I'm celebrating my birthday on August 9th, she has gotten my birthday mixed up with my brother Keith's birthday. His birthday was September 9th. Moving right along, Christmas was so special to me. Mom loved to sing Christmas Carols, especially the Temptations' silent night song. She would decorate the tree so beautifully.

You could see the sparkle in her eyes from the bulbs on the tree. She used to stuff our stockings with the candy, nuts, and oranges. My little sister's stocking was always the biggest, and the most beautiful with her name in glitter. My stocking said Tom on it. I never said anything. I was just grateful to get a stocking. Around Easter time, you couldn't tell me nothing. Mom would make our skirt sets, and she would say baby go to the store so everyone can see you. My older sisters, they called her mama. She dressed to impress.

I started to notice that I wasn't special or noticed because no one ever told me. All the other children were placed on a pedestal, especially the two girls. They were mom's favorite. My youngest brother and I were nine months apart. We used to fight all the time. He was so fat and bad. No one ever wanted to watch him. He would always start with me. My mom would beat the daylights out of me. One time, one of my friends saw me crying when we were going to school, and she called DYFS (Division of Youth and Family Services) on my mom. Mom said to them, "take her." I noticed that she really didn't love me.

I remember my first speedy job. I was so excited to bring a couple of dollars into the house, but to my surprise, my mom would wait for the mailman to make sure I received my check, and after I cashed it, she would leave me with around twenty dollars. Oh my!

We had rats that were bigger than the cats. I remember having rats running all through the house. At night, I used to feel something crawling on me, but I was too scared to look. They would eat up my clothes. I remember one day, mom was in the bathroom, and she said oh no, they are coming through the toilet. Mom was not afraid of anything. She grabbed lye and poured it on the rats in the toilet. All you could hear was the rats screaming like a human. Jesus! When I was eleven years old, I was attracted to the church across the street because the pastor's wife showed me attention. Mom went every once and awhile, and she took me with her.

But most of all, I loved the church dinners that the pastor's wife sold every Saturday. I used to go over there every time the car pulled up. The reverend would send me to the store. Back then, five dollars was a lot of money. The reverend always wanted crackers, a newspaper, and a Pepsi soda. So, every Sunday before I went to church, I would go to the store for them. I even got baptized there, and when I say the water was cold, it really chilled my body and my soul. I never understood what the reverend was speaking about because he used to give out picket numbers and scream from the top of his lungs. After the service, the women would go up in his office.

I remember one Sunday morning mom and I went there, and she put money in the offering plate. She meant to put five dollars, but mistakenly put in fifty dollars. She was so hurt. She has not been back since. Every Sunday I would run over to the church to help them out. It was one sunny summer Sunday, and I went outside, and they called me across the street to go to the store for them. I was so excited because that was an easy five dollars that they gave me. The reverend said get Ritz crackers, a newspaper, and a Pepsi soda. As I write this, I also remembered it was my birthday that day. I couldn't wait to tell them. So, I may get more money.

Well, I came back from the store. I ran out of breath climbing up those big brick steps. I ran inside to give the Reverend his items. He told me to put it inside his office. I never been in his office before. It looked spooky. I put his stuff on his desk. As I was coming out, he was coming in, but when he came in, he locked the door behind him. I thought that was strange. But anyway, this was my only chance to tell him that it's my birthday.

Fish Head & Grits

I was super excited. I said Reverend, here is your change, and guess what it's my birthday. Reverend grabbed me and began to put his hands up my little skirt. Back then, you dare to wear pants in the Lord's house. I never felt so violated in my life. He said let me take you around the corner and lick your rim. I didn't know what rim was back in those days. I ran home and told my mom and dad. The only advice was not to go back over there. Every man that had charge over my life was the very ones that let me down. Who could I turn to?

School was always average for me. No matter how hard I studied, I always got a "C." I knew I could do the work, but no one would push me. Only when I got an "F" was when the switches came out. I was also a class clown as well. I knew that I would get my classmates to like me. One summer, my friend Sylvia and I used to go swimming at the local pool. At the age of fourteen, I was a brick house. I was built like a woman. So, Sylvia and I decided to go swimming with the eighteen years and up crew. I was so down, even though I didn't know how to swim. I just wanted to get into the water, so I had walked around the edge of the pool.

As I was walking around the edge of the pool, this handsome man approached me. He had to be about twenty years old. He asked me did I want to float with him, and I said yes. He lifted me up and told me to wrap my legs around him and we launched out into the deep. I was floating, and so excited that someone wanted to float with me. Suddenly, my bathing suit slides to the side, and I felt something hard penetrating me. I didn't know I was about to get raped. I began to scream, and he stopped and brought me back to the edge of the pool. I won't try to be grown no more.

When I was thirteen years old, my mom treated me like Cinderella. I would always have to clean the house by myself. To my recollection, my mother has three girls and three boys, but I had to do everyone's work. One day mom made a schedule. She said all the girls would have a week a piece, but my other sisters never did their week. Every time I complained that this was their week, my mom made excuses for them. I was always afraid of my mother because she treated me so harsh. So, I did everything to stay on her good side. I remember my oldest sister had a baby and her name is Linda.

She was so beautiful. My oldest sister always worked and kept herself busy. One day, mom told me to watch my niece while my sister went to work and clean up the house or I would get a beating. All this had to be done before she got home. I was thirteen. My niece was two months old. That day, I was overwhelmed with the orders I had. On top of that, we had no hot water. So, I called my friend Sheila to help me. Shelia came over and held the baby while I boiled the water to wash the dishes. When the water was boiling hot, that meant it was ready. I proceeded to pick the pot up with the steam coming from it.

As I picked it up, a little water burned my hand, and I dropped the pot of boiling water. The water hit my friend's foot, and she dropped the baby into the hot water that hit the floor. I rushed over to pick her

Fish Head & Grits

up and all I could see was her skin rolling off her chest. I was devastated. I called my family, and they rushed home. She was in the burn unit for around two to three weeks. The day she came home, I was so happy to see her. The first thing my mom and sister said to me was, "you can't hold her because it's all your fault." Until that day my heart cries.

Baggage. Baggage. Baggage.

I remember my oldest brother was the karate kid. He used to teach me karate. Anytime someone bothered me, I would practice with him. He used to make me do the split and pop my legs. I knew I was tough then. I remember when I was younger, my father got up in the middle of the night, took a stroller and beat my brother with it. He treated him so mean because he had a different father. My brother had to run for his life. He moved in with granny and he was safe there.

Mom used to always call me fast. She used to slap me in the face and leave her handprint on it. Sometimes I got slick, I would hide in the dryer. She could never find me there. But it was when I went to sleep, she would have an extension cord and she would tear me up. My brother (God rest his soul) was damaged by my father. My father would tell my other brother to get the vaseline and gloves and he would bring him in the room and close the door. Now it all makes sense as to why my brother was so mean. I used to love looking at the family picture album because there were so many memories.

Valerie Seymoure

Everyone had missing teeth and a funny hairdo. I noticed that every one of my siblings had a baby picture, but I didn't have one. It was strange that everyone's picture was up there coming straight from the hospital in a blanket. I learned later that I wasn't supposed to be here. They didn't want me. I was a mistake. Grandma told me how I always stayed in the crib and dirty with matted hair. Oh my! So, I was pretty much abandoned from the womb.

FAMILY FIGHT

One year, I watched my family have a fight with the neighbors next door. All I can remember is this lady next door took a bat and hit my dad across the face and blood came gushing out going everywhere. You could hear his head. It sounded like a professional ball player hitting a home run. Mom went upstairs to boil water to throw on the lady. Once the boiling water was ready, mom came out with the pot of water to throw it on her. The lady says to mom, if you throw that water on me, I'm going to really hurt you. It took mom only a few seconds to think about what she was about to do. So, she put the pot down.

Meanwhile, dad had lost his mind. He would come home and throw away all the food. He said it was poisoned. We couldn't go outside or anything. I remember my oldest sister had a toothache and he didn't even care. He wouldn't let us leave the house, but only to go to school and back home. One day my sister and brother went to school and her guidance counselor asked her was everything okay. She said no and told them everything that was going on in the house. All I remember was once I got out of school, I had to pick a few clothes and leave. They took us out of hell and put us in a shelter. Mom seemed a little happier then when we returned after thirty days. My father was taken out of the house. He went into a mental institution.

PIECE BY PIECE

My mom reached out for help to welfare. They came in and gave us a whole new heating system, and I couldn't wait until the first of the month came, because we had food. We didn't have to worry about stuff going in the garbage or fish heads and grits. When mom got on her feet, she was able to rent the apartment on the first floor. It was a Spanish woman with three children. Their ages were two, three, and six years old. My. favorite one was the two-year-old. His name was Randy. He had fat cheeks. He had a head full of curly hair, and a great smile that would light up all outdoors.

RANDY DIES

One morning when I was about to go to school, I heard crying coming from the hallway. As I was going down the stairs, I saw my mother going into the first-floor apartment. I went in behind her and in the crib my little friend was laying there lifeless. His eyes were wide as two silver dollars. His mouth was wide open as if he had saw a ghost. His skin was blue as the sky. I didn't know what had happened, but I was so sad. Come to find out, he was raped by his own grandfather that night and his rectum was busted wide open. The look in his eyes was from shock. My God! And you wonder why I praise Him the way I do. In high school, I was extremely popular, but I didn't know it. Everyone liked the way I dressed, and how I made them laugh.

I remember my sister had a skating party at her school, Rough Riders. I was in the ninth grade at the time. I was skating my hinny off. They had a competition for the best female skater. So, I decided to get in the ring not knowing that all eyes were on me. I was skating to show off going backwards and doing tricks, then the music went off, and the judge said, the winner was Linda's little sister. I'm like, oh snap! I won a trophy with a skate on it. All wasn't bad. When I was fifteen, I met the love of my life. He used to bring me to his house to hang out. His mom loved me. One day his mom came home, and we were caught by her. Shame on me. Six months later, I was pregnant. My mother asked me was I pregnant.

I said to her that I didn't know because she never talked to me about having sex or the birds and the bees. She took me to the doctor to find out if I was pregnant. She said to me, you can't bring no child into this house. So, she took me to an abortion clinic. It was sad to say, but I felt special that day because I was getting attention from my mother. Yay! It lasted for a week, and she went to bring me food and check on me. That was the best feeling in the world. When I turned seventeen, I was in high school.

Fish Head & Grits

I was so serious about getting good grades, and I wasn't taught about going to college. I was always told you almost made it or you're not good enough. I'm in my senior year. I decided to study real hard in spite of what was going on at the house. I started believing in myself. My grades were picking up in school, and I was feeling pretty good about myself.

TEACHER CALLS US FAILURES

One day we were taking our finals and let me tell you something, I really studied hard for that test. The teacher noticed that someone in the class was cheating, and she said everyone put down your pencils. You are all failures.

You will never be nothing. I was so disappointed because I was almost finished with my test knowing that I was going to get an A. That was when the spirit of inadequacy attached itself to me. I died inside that day. Now if mom, dad, the pastor, my friends, and the teacher didn't believe in me, who am I?

I remember another teacher took advantage of me. He told me that I was so beautiful, and I used to go to his house. Well, you know the rest. What lesson did I learn from the teacher?

Valerie Seymoure

PROM

I was so excited about going to the prom, even though I didn't have a dress or a date. At that time, I was dating my daughter's father. He had gotten shot so he couldn't make it. I was able to scrape up some money for our ticket. I ran to give the money to one of the teachers just for her to tell me it was too late. All the seats were taken, and the other slots were for the teachers.

I was so sad, but I didn't give up. Mike's mom gave me a dress she had brought for herself, and I looked amazing. So, we decided that we were going to go anyway. We would show up, but just not eat anything. We had the most amazing time that evening. The teacher came up to me and just looked at me.

After my prom, Mike and I called ourselves going to a hotel. We still had our prom clothes on. The clerk said, come back with your parents, and you can get in. Oh my! I also made Miss senior of the year class in 1986. All these little accomplishments that I could not see because I was looking at the forest and not at the trees.

Fish Head & Grits

GRADUATION

When I walked across that stage, I felt so good. I wanted hugs and kisses but thank God for the diploma. After graduating from high school, I had no ambition. I was afraid of challenging myself because I did not ever want to hear you're not good enough.

Even in those days, it was all there was. No good role models to follow. There were empty fields with broken glasses. There were abandoned buildings. There were drunkards and dope fiends, etc.

Pregnancy was at an all-time high. The women were all on welfare, and it was glamorized. We had food stamps, free checks, and good apartments. This was something that I could get comfortable with. No one was stressing. This was perfect. Nobody was being challenged.

THE BIG EIGHTEEN: ON DRUGS

When I turned eighteen, I met this young lady that accepted me for who I was. I always wanted a friend that was beautiful and that could dress because that was me. On my birthday, she said that I looked so nice, and she wanted me to try cocaine. Mind you, I have never had cocaine.

I took it because I had very low self-esteem and was ready for anything. In addition to that, peer pressure. So, I said okay. I took one sniff, and I didn't understand what I was feeling. Every night I kept taking it. My friend's boyfriend was a dealer. She got the cocaine for free.

Valerie Seymoure

How many know there is nothing in life for free. I wasn't hooked on the drugs, but I was hooked on being accepted. Read that again. Once I stopped hanging around my friend, then I was hooked on the drug.

PREGNANT AGAIN

One day I had gone to the doctor only to find out that I was pregnant again. Twice I was pregnant by my daughter's father. Twice my mother made me get an abortion. But the third pregnancy, she said keep it. Immediately, I stopped using drugs until I had her. Thank the Lord for having mercy and giving me the willpower not to use drugs during my pregnancy.

I picked back up on the drugs when my daughter was two years old. I had a huge family, so I know when I wanted to use, I would take her downstairs and put her in my mother's bed. They loved her. Thank God they were there. Mom used to see me high and beat me. She didn't know that I was dead in the inside.

She didn't know that I needed her more than ever. Mostly everyone in my family used drugs. But I was the bad one. I was the junky. I was the nobody. My brother Keith was so spoiled that he was the biggest addict ever, but my mom saw him as her little prince. I stayed in my addiction for years.

I remember I had about $19.00, and I took it to my dealer, and he wouldn't take it. He said I was short, and I had to see another dealer. It was around 10:30 at night and a man appeared out of nowhere. He said

Fish Head & Grits

to me, what do you need, and I said I'm short. He said I got you. He went into his mouth and gave me a capsule. I gave him the money, and he said he will give me the other one, just stay right there.

So, I stayed there for like 45 minutes, and it hit me that he was not coming back. Oh well, I went back to the house and thought at least I have one. I opened it up, and low and behold, it was chalk. Talk about the donkey face. Every penny I had went to the drug man, but I never messed with mommy's rent. I remember one day, I got slick, and I was switching up bottles on the dealer. Thank God for mercy, because he caught me one day, and said girl give me my cocaine. Back then he could have really hurt me, but God.

Back in the day, my boyfriend sold drugs. He came home one night with ten clips and put them into the microwave and left back. It was on and popping. I tell you, I sniffed two clips in one night, and I refilled each cap with aspirin.

Valerie Seymoure

ARRESTED

I knew I was going to get it then. So, I signed myself into a detox program just to get away from him because I knew I was dead meat. In the detox program they said that they had no room for me because cocaine wasn't a problem. So, my problem still stood. I remember I gave all my underwear away because the girls came with nothing but the clothes on their backs. I remember being in the meeting and the girls called me a people pleaser. This hurt my heart so bad because I thought I was helping them.

After the detox, I came home only to start off where I finished. I got a job working in the medical field. I remember one day I was on my way to work, and I went to buy my drugs to take to work. A next-door neighbor gave me a ride to go cop. I saw my dealer and got out of the car and asked him to give me two. They were the long glass capsules. He gave me two and just plucked them down.

When I plucked them, I noticed that they were only halfway full. I went back to my dealer, and said, "Hey, this is only a half full." He looked at me and said that it's not his. Back then I was a rookie in the drug game. As I argued with him, he had a look of terror in his eyes. Two cars pulled up right behind me, and they got out and they began talking on their walkie talkies. They said just the girl and John. So, I put the capsules in my mouth, and they put me in one cop car and John in the other. They put the cuffs on me. Oh my!

Fish Head & Grits

As we were riding down to the police station, I asked the cops, "Why do you have me in the car?" He noticed that I had something in my mouth. So, he pulled the car over and tried to take it out of my mouth. By the time he got to the backseat, I had swallowed both capsules. He said if you swallowed the glass bottles of cocaine, the glass could cut up your arteries and the cocaine will freeze up your heart. I was so scared that I told him the truth. He rushed me to the hospital, and they began to pump my stomach. They gave me something to bring the capsules up.

Everything had come up. My dinner from that night, my breakfast from this morning, but the capsules would not come up. They took x-rays and they saw two long objects in my throat on a slant. My God! After the hospital, they took me to the police station because I had no identification on me. They wanted to lock me up. I called my daughter's grandmother to bring me my ID so they wouldn't.

I had that one phone call to make. As I was finishing up the paperwork at the jail house, the officer told me to take my shoestrings out my shoes. By the time I finished taking them both, Sarah was there with my ID. I was so happy that I never got to see the inside of the jail cell. I was a free woman.

As I entered the threshold going out, it was like the Channel 2 news was out there. Sarah brought my family and hers too. I was so hurt, embarrassed and full of shame. They all said mean things to me. If that wasn't enough, they brought my daughter also. She was only two years old at that time. They told her to look at her horrible mother. They said I was no good. They called me a jail bird. I never lived that down anytime I went to her house. I was the talk of the house. That hurt me to see my daughter. I couldn't understand why the capsule wouldn't come up, but when I think back on it now, if it would have come up, I wouldn't have a good job. I tell you what an amazing God we serve. Even in your mess, God will hide you. I am just a miracle. Halleluiah! Moving forward, you would think that all I been through, I would stop taking the drugs.

I didn't know how to stop. One day I was buying my drugs from this guy, and he showed me a little attention. He asked me if I wanted to hang out after I got off from work. I said yes. I was not a street person, and I definitely wasn't street smart. So, after work, he picked me up that evening. I thought I was cute, and I was going to get high for free.

We sniffed around three capsules together, and he began to kiss on me. I was not down with that mess. He became angry with me, and I told him I didn't want to have sex. He told me he wasn't going to give me a ride home if I didn't sleep with him and he said he was going to call all his boys to rape me, and I was out of there.

I was so paranoid, and my heart was racing so fast you could see it through my blouse. I made it to the corner, then I saw the bus stop. I took a deep breath and thought I was free. Then, I heard someone calling me. It was him. He was in his car trying to convince me to get in. As I ignored him, he got out of his car and came up to me and punched me in my eye. Even though it was still dark outside, I saw stars. He lit my whole world up. He got back in his car and took off. The bus finally pulls up and I got on holding my eye for dear life. But I still continued to use after that incident. What would it take for me to get it? Every time my mother saw me high, she would hit me.

So, I used to creep up the stairs. My brother Keith used to get high as a kite, and she never bothered him. My brother loved to sew his own clothes and his own sneakers. He was the jack of all trades. He loved music and going out to the clubs. He was always fat and juicy looking, but because of the use of drugs, he became very thin.

My other brother hated me so much that he tried to hold me down and put bleach down my throat. I was so afraid of him. He was the bully of the house. He took everything from everyone. Now that I look back, he was really crying out from what was taken from him which was his innocence. Wow! My oldest sister lived on campus, and she got out of the house, and made something of herself.

My baby sister was so beautiful. Mom dressed her like she played on 90210. She was sharp from her head to her toes. She was very smart as well. She always had trouble in school because of the way she dressed and looked. One day she wore my leather skirt set to school, and she didn't hardly make it halfway through her morning classes. She was beat up so bad. Mom had to put her into private school.

Valerie Seymoure

MEETING GOD

I remember the church folk used to come on the street telling you to get right with God. They used to tell me you are going to hell. They would show me in the word all my sins. So, I was afraid of God. I thought of God as this big mean God; ready to destroy you if you don't change. It was a no for me. I didn't want no parts of God. They never told me that God loved me. One New Year's Eve, I was waiting for the ball to drop. I had my cocaine and my cigarettes getting it in. My eyes were as wide as two basketballs, and my mouth did an uncontrollable movement.

Twerking is what they call it today. Years later, I found out that mouth movement was really a mini stroke. My God! When the ball dropped, I was skeed out of my brain. I had an 8 ball, which is a lot of cocaine. When the ball dropped on the TV that night, people on the set was saying happy new year's. Even though I was high, I still knew how to celebrate. Right at that moment, God began to speak to me. He said, "I kept you because I love you." Oh my!

Tears began to run down my cheek, and I said to Him, "you love me." But in my heart, I knew no one loved me. I told God that I was going to give him a try, but with my hand pointed in the air, I said, "But if you don't work, I'm out of here." Oh, how sweet it is to turn your life over to God. At that moment his presence took over me. I had no more desire to use. He took the taste out of my mouth instantly.

Fish Head & Grits

POST OFFICE TEST

But before I stopped using, I had to take a test for a job. That night before taking the drug test, I found some drugs behind my dresser. I did not know the test was the next day. I went anyway and took the test. The test came back negative. When you are in God's hands, he will make a way out of no way. The Lord began to tell me what to do. He told me to tell the young lady that has been battling with drug addiction that she's a diamond in the rough. One morning I was by SNS, and she was out there begging for change. She would hold the door for you. I told her that God said she was a diamond in the rough, and God wanted to help her. I told her that I would help her get clean.

FIRST MINISTRY

I told her how God changed my life. Sometimes you must be transparent to help others. Two weeks later, she called me. She was ready for a new life. That morning I woke up at around 5 a.m. to go pick her up. As I entered the hallway, she was under the staircase of the house laying down.

There was food, clothes, and other stuff around her. I told her let's go. So, she tried to take some of that mess with her, but I told her that she was going to have a brand-new life. So, she left her remaining goods and got in the car. As I was driving, she laid her head in my lap, and said, "you care."

Valerie Seymoure

I said to her, "I sure do." She was ninety pounds soaking wet. After thirty days, I went to visit her, and she was fifty pounds heavier. I didn't know who she was, but she knew who I was. She ran to me and picked me up and spent me around. She literally swept me off my feet. The joy in her heart became contagious. She was able to get all the help she needed. However, she had many other issues. She was homeless, she was HIV and AIDS positive, and recovering from addiction.

As I think back on how all these things were a part of my ministry, I realized that God was setting the stage. I remember God told me to volunteer at the University Hospital. When I went to volunteer, they sent me straight to the Chapel office. I never told them that I was even a Christian. I just showed up. They said I didn't have any credentials so maybe I could answer the phones. At around this time I had applied for an apartment, which came four weeks later.

I finally had my own apartment. I noticed everyone loved coming to my place to eat and talk to me. Most of them had HIV/AIDS. I treated them like family. I remember one of my friends having it, and I brought her to my mother's house.

My mother told me to never bring that diseased girl back to her house. Weeks later, we noticed my brother Keith was kind of losing his mind. He said to us that we weren't nothing. I didn't quite understand what he meant. We also noticed that he had lost a tremendous amount of weight.

Fish Head & Grits

Being that he used drugs, we thought he lost the weight from that. A couple of days later, mom gets a call from the hospital to talk to them about her son. Back then, AIDS was a body eating disease. Everybody was scared to be around anyone that had it. So, we went up there to see him and they told us that he had AIDS and was in his last stage. He spent his last days at the house in his room. I would go up to his room and read him scriptures out of the Bible. I don't remember what I was saying but God did.

I put a little cross on his chest. He was able to talk, but he couldn't walk anymore. I bought him some bedroom shoes that he liked. He told me that he will walk again. Every day I went upstairs to talk to him and make him laugh. When my father heard the news of my brother Keith's illness, he came and took Keith in his arms downstairs and put him into the bathtub. He was so angry at Keith because he had contracted this disease. He was treating Keith so roughly while he was in the tub and was crying out until my mom had to take over.

Every day I went to see Keith, I saw the slippers across the room, and I said, he will wear them one day. My mother didn't have much to say about my friend anymore, because the very thing she rejected was in her own house. This was totally a different story. One day while I was working at the Post Office in Newark, I received a phone call from my mom. That was strange. I left everything and rushed home. When I arrived at the house, my mother was in a panic. She told me to go upstairs to see about Keith. I knew deep in my heart that he had died.

Valerie Seymoure

So, I went upstairs and opened the door to his room, and I saw him lying on the floor with his eyes rolled back in his head. Foam was coming out of his mouth. I called his name, but there was no response. I did notice that he had his cross still on his chest. The paramedics came and took him.

They covered him with a white sheet. I was devastated. My mom was sad, and she didn't know what to do. I thank God for allowing me to be the strong one in the family. "God's power is made perfect in weaknesses." 2 Corinthians 12:9. God made me strong. It was a sad day when Keith went away.

My prayers changed. I began praying and thanking God for keeping my mom through the whole process. Now my friend had started getting sick. Her mom had called me and told me that her daughter was sick and that she refused to get into the ambulance to receive help. She asked if I could come over and see about her. I did, and I went with her to the hospital. She looked at me and saw me crying. When I saw her, I saw death on her face. She started hyperventilating saying she was going to die. I had to get it together so she could feel safe. When we got to the hospital, I encouraged her that she was not going to die. They were able to treat her right away. As they were taking blood from her, she had touched my hand. Lions, tigers, and bears, oh my! What was I supposed to do? She said if you're my sister, you wouldn't mind. The devil is a liar! Thank God for his word, "No weapon that is formed against you shall prosper;" Isaiah 54:17.

28

Fish Head & Grits

However, I was still volunteering at the hospital answering phones. It was fun, and I loved going there being a part of God's plan.

UNIVERSITY HOSPITAL: TRAINING

I was told that I would be trained to go on the floor. I said okay. I was excited. The training was amazing; knowing that I already had hands on training with my family and friends, I would not be surprised at what I would encounter through this training. When the training was over, I was sent on the floor to minister. They sent me to the AIDS ward. I had introduced myself to some of the women on the ward. I prayed with them and ministered to them and to do what I do best by making them laugh. But most importantly, I listened to their problems.

I went from room to room with so much joy in my heart. It was a piece of cake until I entered one room that had two men in there. So, I knocked on the door and went in to introduce myself. To the first young man, I prayed for him and encouraged his heart. I looked on the other side of the curtain and I saw death, and I began to think about my brother Keith. The man looked to be about 6 feet and 5 inches, and he was all skin and bones. There was blood around the man's mouth and his right arm was in a sling. His hair was as straight as a baby's. It stuck straight in the air. His eyes were glassy, and he could barely blink. I told God I would have to pray for him while I'm walking.

This brought back too many memories. But wait a minute, as I was walking out of the room, God told me to go back and pray with him.

He said for me to decrease so he could increase. So, I went back in and prayed the sinner's prayer with him. So, I asked the young man if he heard me to please blink or move his hand that was in the sling. He did nothing. So, as I proceeded to walk out of the room, the Holy Spirit said look back, and I saw the man wiggle his fingers. I was so in "awe" with God. He did good. I was so glad that I was able to lead that man to salvation.

ADOPTING RALPH

Now that I have my new apartment, more people who confided in me had AIDS. They would come over to my place and eat and sing, just to have a good time. I loved going to minister at the hospital. I would bring gifts, and clothing for the patients. I loved to sing to them too. One day I had gotten a phone call, and they said that my friend had died. There were no plans to have her repast, so I had it at my apartment. My friend's mother had her two kids, but she could not care for them. So, I took the youngest one to give her a break.

He gave me such a hard time. I just wanted to love him because he didn't have his mom anymore. I took care of him for at least one year. He acted up so bad that I did not have any control over him. Unfortunately, I had to give him back because DYFS (Division of Youth and Family Services) were prying into my business. They were trying to make something bad out of a good situation. They gave me such a hard time with him and told me that I was unfit to care for him. It was hurtful for the both of us.

MY NEW HOUSE

Around this time, I had bought my new house and allowed everyone to come and stay with me. When I was in my house up in my attic, I was hanging up some clothes and heard something strange. It scared me and I said don't panic.

I said if I hear it again, then I'm out of here. So, I continued to hang up my clothes only to hear that strange sound again. I was out of there. I called somebody to come and pray in my house because I didn't know any ghostbusters.

HELPING PROSTITUTES IN THE STREET

My next mission was to help the prostitutes in the streets. I was working the night shift, and I had got off at 2:30 in the morning. I would see many women in the streets, and it would be freezing cold. They had on these little toosy skirts practically showing their behinds. I felt so bad for them. I started picking these ladies up and bringing them into my home. My home was a place for them to have a bath, a decent meal, and somewhere to sleep. In the morning, I took them to a drug free program. Only God could give such a mission as that. Me and my daughter never got hurt, and no one stole anything from me. That was all the plan of God.

Valerie Seymoure

You can't do nothing like that today because people have changed. However, I still will provide food and clothing for them and a reasonable shelter where they can attend. One day at the hospital, I met a pastor that loved the work that I was doing, and he says to me that he would like me to help him minister and he brought me to the boarding home. At that time the boarding homes were for the AIDS patients. When I entered the building, a big bird cage stood before me. Everything in the place was so beautiful. I looked so grand. I was on a mission, and I was trained and equipped to do such great work.

I started by going on Sundays with another pastor. He would have the room full of people singing and praising and testifying about God. I also served the people communion. A year later that pastor had died, and the mantle was passed down to me. So, during the week, I would go and pay them a visit. I would go from room to room praying with them and bringing a listening ear. I used to bring them clothes and goodies, but the one thing I enjoyed was to see them smile. It made my heart smile. Some rooms that I had went to were so grateful for me praying for them that they end up praying for me.

Fish Head & Grits

BROADWAY HOUSE

I have learned that you must form a relationship with people before you start preaching to them the gospel. I would go from room to room spreading love and joy, but the people needed me to lift their spirits. I would sing to them and make them laugh, which was the best medicine ever. I had to earn their trust, and the only way I was able to do that was to be who God called me to be.

After about four years into this ministry at the Broadway House, the manager came to me and asked me can I do a service for the people. I said yes, and from then on, my ministry went to another level. The Holy Spirit in me would light up the darkest soul.

I was trying to make friends with a young woman and when I approached her, she said to me, "poof be gone." I really had the donkey face then, but I didn't stop trying. After two more visits, she was like puddy in my hands. I would get to the Broadway house before service starts to encourage the people to come. After a while, the word got around the building that Minister Valerie is funny and that she loves and accepts everyone.

At first there were only four people coming to the service every week. Every day I went to visit the residents. There was a young lady that was looking incredibly sad. So, I asked her what the matter was, and she said it was her birthday. She said no one came to see her or bought her any presents. I felt her pain. That took me back to when I was a little girl and never had a birthday party. God has a way of making your misery your ministry. I told her to stay right there, and I will be right back. I had thirteen dollars to my name, and I went to the bakery store and bought her a cake with her name on it. When I gave her the cake, her eyes lit up and the smile on her face showed every tooth in her mouth.

BIRTHDAY CELEBRATION

The young lady that I bought the cake for invited a lot of the residents to come and get a piece of her cake. This birthday celebration opened the door for Beauty for Ashes. So, once a month, whoever's birthday it was, Beauty for Ashes celebrated the persons birthday with a cake and gifts.

We would have such a great time. After the service, I would hang around and visit the new residents. I did not know that I was working in the gift of pastoring. I didn't know my job was to win souls for Christ and to have them cross over. This was so amazing that the people at their last breath would give their life to Christ. Hallelujah!

At one point they were bringing their financial offerings. Every week the Holy Spirit would give me new ideas to keep them excited. We made them deacons and sisters of the church. The Lord was performing miracles like crazy. There was a guy in the house that I would call my buddy, and he was blind. He had to be escorted into the service by an aid. One night I went into an all-night prayer on his behalf because his prayer was to see. Thank God that the room became packed every week. So, one night my daughter came to assist with the service. We opened with praise and worship, and then testimony time. Everyone had gone around the room. My buddy came forward to testify. He says I want to tell you what a beautiful pink shirt you have on, and I said thank you. And as he was testifying, it hit me, and I said wait a minute.

I replied to him, "you know what color I have on?" He said yes, and he described me from head to toe. We couldn't do nothing but give God praise for the miracle of restoring my buddy's sight. Halleluiah! Because of the presence of Beauty for Ashes at the Broadway, there was a senior citizen man who came to visit the services at my church. I would go and pick him up every Sunday and bring him to church.

At around this time, I was in a relationship. The relationship wasn't going too well. It was very bad. He was mistreating me, and I allowed it to happen, because I wanted to be loved. When God convicted me of my sins, I changed. I wanted to look good when I went into the church. I wanted to get married and have the house with the picket fence.

AIDS

I remember when I was around my 20's, I just got saved but I wasn't sanctified. My boyfriend came home, and he planned on marrying me. For thirty days we were like rabbits doing everything under the sun. After the thirty days, he left me. He packed all his things and moved to

Valerie Seymoure

Georgia. I was devastated. So, I decided in my little Peewee brain that if I go down to visit him, he'd come back to me and my daughter. Lo and behold, I took a plane down there. I figured if he seen my daughter and I, he'll know how much we loved him, and he will come back home to us.

Come to find out he was in a mental institution which really didn't matter to me. I just wanted to hear the magic words that he'll be back. Once we arrived, I began to walk down the hall with my daughter clinching her hand real tight. I was both excited and nervous. When I saw him, he came out and we just began to talk. I was waiting for the magic words. After the visit, it was like a bulb went off in my head. That little, small voice saying something's not right. Back then, I really didn't know God, but he knew me. I decided to go to the nurse's desk, and I asked her why Michael was here, and she said everything in here is confidential.

So, I said okay. I'll respect that and I begin to walk down the hall with my daughter. As my daughter and I was walking down the hall, that same nurse catches up with me and she is out of breath, and she grabs my arm and said please don't say anything because I can lose my job and I said not a problem. She said to me in a disturbing voice he's here because he has AIDS. When God is taking something from you, trust Him. It's for your own good. By the grace of God, I did not contract HIV nor AIDS.

Fish Head & Grits

MARRIED TO THE WORLD

I got married to a new guy and now everything is in order, so I thought. In my heart, I knew he didn't love me because he didn't even love himself. I stayed with him for ten years. I was being mentally, verbally, and physically abused by my husband. I couldn't see it because I learned in the church that a sanctified wife will sanctify her husband. So, I stayed in the marriage believing that one day my husband would change. Christmas came around, and I was looking to get a gift from my husband. He neither told me Merry Christmas nor gave me a gift.

So, we went to church and picked up one of the clients from the Broadway House to take him there. He was paralyzed from the waist down, and we had to lift him up to put him into the van along with his wheelchair. Moving forward, when we arrived at the building, my husband spoke to everyone and wished them a Merry Christmas. I was so hurt because he didn't acknowledge me at all. So, we took Mike and pushed him to the back of the church which is where he felt comfortable.

We went to sit in the front where we sat at every Sunday to hear the preacher. I was so sad because I didn't receive any gifts from my husband or any kind of acknowledgement from him. The pastor had called up all the women that he wanted to thank except me. So, I was really feeling abandoned and hurt.

Valerie Seymoure

Just when the service was about to be almost over, God shows up in an unexpected way. I heard someone yell my name with a loud voice from the back, and says, "I have a gift for Valerie." Everyone looked to the back, and it was Mike in his wheelchair. Mike stood up and put his wheelchair brakes on and proceeded to take step by step down the aisle, saying that this gift is for you. Merry Christmas. Everyone in the church was astonished. All I could do was fall on my knees and worship God.

God has given me a gift that couldn't be wrapped. He did it just for me. After that, my heart was filled with joy. That was the best gift. I haven't seen Mike walk since that service. Meanwhile, my husband was still abusing me and told me that I was fat and that no one would want me. I was so afraid of him. If he was to just move his hand, I would jump and flinch.

One day, he had asked me for some money, and I told him no, and he threw me all around the house. I didn't have sense to understand or know that I was being abused until I went to a class at Essex County College. This class helped me a great deal, so that I was able to help other women like me. Everything that was taught in the class was about my abuse. God seems to always have a way of showing me up. I've come to realize that I must get out of this abusive relationship.

The abuse was getting worse until I had to call the police. The police came and told me to get a restraining order against him. I went and did that just to allow him to come back in. What's a girl to do? Crazy! Well, the abuse went on for a long time, but in different ways that I couldn't even imagine.

We had just come back from shopping at the grocery store, and he had gotten out of the car and went and sat on the back porch. I sat in the car feeling some type of way. He asked me if I had any money, and I said no. He started to hit me, but he thought about being arrested by the police. So, he hawk spit at me right in my face, and all I could do was wipe my face as the saliva came running down my cheeks. He took the abuse to another level, and I still stayed in my marriage.

THE LAST STRAW

The last straw was when my friend Bernice told me the truth. She says, "Valerie, he doesn't love you." When she said that, it penetrated my heart. She told me if I stayed in the marriage, it's going to hurt me. If I get out of the marriage it was going to hurt me too. My heart. I remember what the words says about a friend. "The kisses of an enemy may be profuse, but faithful are the wounds of a friend." Proverbs 27:6. She told me to get a lawyer, and I pressed to get a lawyer and started the process.

The day of the divorce, I still had a glimmer of hope that he might change. That morning of the divorce, I had a change of heart. I didn't want to get a divorce. The lawyer told me that the only way the divorce would be granted is if I tell a lie. In my mind that was my big chance to stay married, because I was not a liar. So, I went before the judge, and he asked me two questions: my name and my address. Once the gavel went down, I was divorced. You see, the Lord will do for you what you can't do for yourself.

AFTER DIVORCE

As I was coming out of the courthouse, I had a vision I was coming out of mud and there were so many people in white clothing pulling me out. They wiped me down and put a white robe on me. After weeks have passed, I felt so disappointed because I had no one. I was upset with my friend because I felt like she had somebody, and I didn't. The devil sure knew how to mess with my mind back then.

Moving right along, I was single all over again, but this time single and broken. My self-esteem shot down and I was feeling worthless and insecure. I manage to take all my baggage that I allowed people to give me. I was weighed down with nowhere to turn. The house was very quiet. I was used to living in dysfunction. So, I decided to give God a real try because I always trusted Him with everything except my relationships. Every time I got into a relationship, I just wanted God to help them but really, I needed help. Thus, I decided to really open my Bible and began to read it. I cried out to the Lord about all my hurts.

The Bible says, "Draw near to God, and he will draw near to you," James 4:8

Fish Head & Grits

RECONCILING WITH MY DAUGHTER

As a mom, I always tried to raise my daughter the best to my knowledge. I remember always going to church with my daughter and and having fun. I really allowed the church to raise her because I was so busy with my last relationship, I couldn't see my daughter with a broken heart. I was so busy trying to take care of a man that was broken as well.

The church even told me if I had to choose between my daughter and my husband who would I choose and I said my daughter. They say wrong, you are supposed to choose your husband because you guys are one and you can always get another daughter, so I lived as such because I thought that was in the will of God.

When she was around 16 years old, I remember me and her used to always sleep together but on this particular night, we were in the bed watching TV and the tampon commercial came on. I knew that my daughter was a virgin. I asked the most ridiculous question, are you pregnant? She said in a soft voice, I don't know…

Immediately, I popped up and jumped into my car. I began to drive down 280. I did not know how to process this at first. I thought in my mind and in my heart that she had to get an abortion because I am too young to be a grandma, then I remember going to work and just battling with God.

I just stopped fighting and accepted that I will be a grandmother. Once I accepted it, she called me at choir rehearsal, and she said ma something fell in the toilet as I was using the church's bathroom. I said baby I'm on my way. I took her to the hospital, and they had to give her a DNC. She lost the baby that night. The next morning, I stayed with her and the nurse was cleaning her up but as I was watching the nurse, the Holy Spirit began to speak to me.

Saying, I gave you that child so you can raise and part greatness in her. I began to cry like a baby. After the nurse left, I went to her bedside, and began to repent! I cried out to God and told my daughter how sorry I was because I didn't treat her like she was supposed to be treated and God showed me how much of a hypocrite that I was. My daughter and I cried together, and our relationship changed from then on. Thank God for the Holy Spirit and Thank God for forgiveness.

Fish Head & Grits

CAR ACCIDENT

As a woman of God, I still had some struggles. I was taught to hate white folks. I was shown movies that made my heart harden towards them. I used to go to work and stop speaking to them. One day, I went to Ponderosa in West Orange – an all you can eat buffet.

Man, I used to love those chicken wings.

When I finished eating, I got into my car and began to drive down the mountain. My car went out of control due to black ice. Suddenly, it hit the divider and began to flip over. Every time the car would flip, the roof of the car would scrape my head. The car flipped five times and skid five-thousand feet. I was dangling upside down from the seatbelt. All I could think was, is this car going to blow up? I unlatched the seatbelt and began crawling across 280.

Cars were coming but none hit me. On the other side was a Caucasian lady waiting for me with a blanket. She wrapped the blanket around me and laid me on the ground. She took out her cell phone and began to call the ambulance. Before they arrived, she also asked me if have any family that she wanted me to call but my family wasn't in town. Five minutes later, the same Caucasian lady comes into my hospital room and says I've watched your car flip five times and I just wanted to come and make sure that you were okay.

She also waited for me because I didn't have a ride home. The lady gave me a ride home and she called me the next day. She even made me a necklace of ivory and onyx. It was a lion. She told me that I was from the tribe of Judah. I had no idea what that meant. Weeks later, I had to go to court because my registration and insurance expired. I was afraid because I knew I was going to jail. On the day of court, a Caucasian prosecutor said to me I'm going to take your case last. I'm going to ask the judge to be lenient on you. Wow!!!!!

To my surprise, when it was my turn, I approached the bench. A Caucasian judge looks over and says how may I help you. I told him what happened, and he asked me did I have any other problems. I told him I had all my information in the car when the towing company told me that I would have to pay three grand to receive all my personal belongings out of the vehicle. The judge gets a piece of paper and began to write on it. He gave me a fine slap on the wrist. Thank you Lord! He wrote me a letter to take to the towing company and the letter reads as follows: "Please release all property out of the vehicle without paying anything." The judge signed it.

I took the note to the towing company, and they told me that they didn't have a green Camry there. The young man walks by as I was speaking, and he said: "Oh you mean the green Camry right there." God will always show up and show out and he had no other choice but to release all my personal belongings. The Lord began to speak to me and say my love is no color. Look at the flowers, they are all different shapes sizes and colors, and they all grow together. That's the same way I want you to love everyone the way I love you. My life changed from then on.

Fish Head & Grits

You can't say you love and have hate in your heart. Thank you Lord for a heart transplant!

ME & MY HUSBAND: A TRUE LOVE STORY

I remember going shopping to a store downtown and I went into the Salvation Army which is my favorite store. I'm a very friendly person and I speak to everyone. On this particular morning, I'm checking out the blouses in one of the aisles. I see this young man and I say good morning with such a big smile and cheer in my heart. The young man responded with "Hi" in such a sad voice. I asked him what was wrong, and he said that his brother was in a coma and didn't know if he was going to make it.

So, I did what I do best by grabbing this young man's hands and beginning to pray in the name of Jesus. I also gave him my phone number just to encourage him 3 days later. He calls me and says my brother is out of the coma with such happiness. The young man asked me which church I belonged to. He began to come every Sunday. He was so excited.

The young man asked me if he could take me out for dinner and I responded with sure. So, every Sunday after service, he would take me out to dinner. After two months, he would come in and be so excited about the things of God. He clapped with joy in his heart, and I was amazed. One morning, the young man even joined the church. He would come over sometime just to talk. One time, he gave me the biggest hug and he smiled so hard. So, I said what's the smiling for? He said I felt your heart beating. How beautiful! I thought no one would ever tell me something like that. What I love about God is that he didn't allow me to see this man as a boyfriend. God had my eyes blinded even though we went to church together every Sunday.

One Sunday, he asked me to come to his church. I never knew he went to church before coming to Chosen. He also wanted me to meet his parents which I thought was amazing. As we're driving down to Neptune, we stopped at the beach. It was dark. The wind was blowing this night and the Moon was just beautiful. He asked me to get up on the lifeguard chair and we sat there and watched the moon. I went to his mom house, and I met his parents.

The first day she brought me an outfit. His parents loved me. I went to visit Jonathan's church and to my surprise, when I saw that man go over to a worship with tears in his eyes and praying over folks, I was blown away. I did not know he was truly a man of God. He respected me enough to say we won't have sex until we get married, whoa! Always remember ladies, however a man treats his mother is how he is going to treat you, so he treated his family with lots of love and respect.

She raised a great son. I remember one day being in church and Jonathan would leave out for a minute. He came back and I smelled smoke on him. I said brother, you smoke? He was like yeah but it's going to be my last cigarette. Mind you, Jonathan hasn't smoked since that day, which was about eleven years ago.

Fish Head & Grits

To God be the glory! See when a man really loves you, he will change. I'm a witness. One week, I didn't see Jonathan come to church. Then the second week, I didn't see Jonathan but the third week, he rose like Jesus when he came to church and said that he couldn't eat, sleep, or breathe without me. He then asked me to marry him. Wow!

When somebody loves you, it doesn't take a million years. We were married within six months. I asked Jonathan why you never try to make love to me before we got married, he said I made love to you the first day I met you. I prayed for you. I prayed that God will send me a wife and he sent you. Now, is John perfect? No…

John is the pain in the toes sometimes, but does he love God? Yes, and that's the difference because God loved me through my husband. John has a past as well. He was arrested many times in his past, but he had a praying family, and he was rooted in the word as a child. His life was spoken over that he would become one of God's servants and today, hubby helps so many people.

He may not do it in the church, and he may not minister the way I do, but John sure has touched hearts all over the world. He used to be 252 lbs. but when he turned fifty, he said he would be in the best shape of his life today. Now he's 175 lbs. because he put in the work and that's one of his gifts that he gives back to the world. He makes videos and has met so many superstars as well.

Valerie Seymoure

It's so funny because he sends videos all day and it could be aggravating sometimes but he doesn't mean no harm. He just wants to bless others. I love the way he prays over others.

FORGIVING MY DAD

Even after all I've been through, I still allowed my father to move into my house. Sometimes, he would help me with my daughter. He used to help me pay the bills in my house. At one point, he stopped paying me to live there and I was devastated. I was a single mom trying to make ends meet and he didn't care. I decided to put him out. I took him to court and the judge gave him 24 hours to move. About a year later, my sister and Mom said let's go find daddy, he was in the shelter up the street.

He acknowledged me only, saying I knew you were going to come back to get me. Dad asked me if he could move back home, and I said yes. That was my way of saying I forgive you and I love you. One morning, he asked me to take him to the bus stop so he can go to work. Five minutes later, he called me back and asked me to pick him up. That's when I knew something was wrong.

Dad was dealing with prostate cancer. He was too stubborn to go to the hospital. He was convinced to go to the hospital and gave me a call that night and asked me to bring him money for the TV and the phone. The next day, I brought money for everything and even bought him a teddy bear. He loved teddy bears. I went to his room, and he wasn't there. The nurse said that he was still downstairs being tested. They asked me to come back maybe within an hour, so I went home and just relaxed. A half-hour later, my mom called me and told me that dad passed away. I was so hurt that I couldn't give him his teddy bear and card. I was just grateful that I was able to make amends with my dad. All glory to God, I am thankful that he gave me the chance to make it right. You see love goes a long way. It's not how people threat you, it's how you respond.

MOM IN THE NURSING HOME

Before we got married, I would always go up to the nursing home to visit my mom. Chantel brought Mama a beautiful dress. She was going to be at the wedding with a sparkling silver dress. But just a week before the wedding, mom got so sick she couldn't even walk. We were saddened by the fact that she couldn't come to the wedding, but right after the wedding, Jonathan and I went up to the nursing home still in our wedding clothes.

All the nurses and doctors and CNAs and the patients just looked like, wow you guys are looking amazing. As we approached my mom's room, she sits up in her bed and says wow you guys look beautiful. I knew she was happy for us.

All that time and God was still working in our relationship. You see, every time I used to go visit my mom, she treated me like I was nothing. I didn't exist.

Valerie Seymoure

She didn't know my name and I was just sick and tired of going up there because she didn't even acknowledge me, so one day I was on the elevator, and I was talking to God. I asked him, I said God… why doesn't my mom want to be bothered with me? I don't want to come back up here anymore because of the way she's treating me, and God spoke to me.

He said that I'm showing you what forgiveness look like. This is the way you treat me. This is the way the world treats me, and I forgive them every day. You see, love and forgiveness doesn't have a limit and after God spoke to me, I went up there a couple of days later to visit her in the morning.

When I walked into her room, she jumped up and said pray. I said mom you want me to pray for you? She said yes. I began to pray for her and asked if she wanted to accept Jesus as her Lord and Savior and she said yes. From that day on, her whole life changed. I was able to take her out of the nursing home and bring her on picnics. I would walk her around the park and kiss her face. This was something that I always wanted to do, and God granted me everything I wanted from my mother as a child.

I was even able to take her to Florida to meet her great grandkids which she never met before. When I tell you God will change your life, I mean it. If you just listen and be obedient to his will, you will receive what you're wishing for. The same dress my daughter brought Mom for my wedding was the same dress that Mom went to glory in. WHO KNEW!!!

Valerie Seymoure

AUTHENTIC SELF

All my life, I knew that I was different and that's why I faced so many attacks. I thought I had to have a degree to be perfect. My experience made me perfect. My heavenly father qualified me. I didn't have to join no group, compromise my integrity, sell out, buy my way or any of it. I've learned that God isn't looking for perfection but for a relationship and someone to do his will. Only then, I was able to find the real Valerie. Hallelujah! I'm a masterpiece of God.

I used to always try to fit into everybody's box. But today, I can't be contained. Glory to God. Remember when man says you're not good enough, then you need to rejoice. That's when God comes in and shows up and shows out. Count it all joy!!! Also remember that every word God said about me is true. Be your authentic self and God will HONOR that. No one can take that from you or duplicate it.

Today, I'm the CEO of my own company – Beauty for Ashes. The Lord has used this ministry to save and change many lives. I was the first partaker and now I am the president. We are worldwide, reaching every nationality.

Be ready for part two!

Made in the USA
Middletown, DE
12 April 2023

28596301R00031